Haiku

A Shoji Screen

Philippe R Hebert

ISBN: 978-81-19654-82-6

First Edition: 2024

Rs. 200/-

Cyberwit.net

HIG 45 Kaushambi Kunj, Kalindipuram

Allahabad - 211011 (U.P.) India

http://www.cyberwit.net

E-mail: info@cyberwit.net

Printed at Repro.

Table of Contents

Shoji screen reveals
White heron motionless hunts
Marshy pond at dusk

A shoji screen
White egret and blue heron
Hunting marshy pond

Sun barely touches
It's magnificent
A purple orchid

Origami swan
So delicate and fragile
Natures bird

A maid in getas
Sweeps the earthen floor again
No need its already clean

Traditions endure
Feudal Japan or today
Who is to say

The tatamies closed
The room is scoured yet again
It can’t be too clean

Yakatori house
Fussa in December
Snow and hot sake

An origami
Takes center stage in the house
Master is coming

Hot bath piles of quilts
An old Japanese hotel
In January

Where dahlias grow
There was a bridge and
a lonely heart sat

El condor passa
oh how majestic in flight
carrion eater

A tropical beauty
swaying in the sun
an invitation

Scent of jasmine
you are whispers of my heart
and shouts in my brain

Pouring forth my heart
and emptying of my soul
how freeing it is

White with yellow are
Calla Lilies portend much
life birth death

A black dahlia
signifies death to all
unfair to dahlias

Blue orange yellow
a bird of paradise
sends a message

Foot path over a bridge
Meet you where the dahlias grow
You wait in vain.

Bio

Philippe R Hebert is an 80 year old poet, writer, and story teller.

- Book of Vietnam War poems “Elephant Ears and Bamboo Shoots” published by Human Error Publishing
- Poetry Book “A Begging Bowl” to be published in 2024 with Human Error Publishing
- Poetry Chapbook in manuscript form “A Saffron Robe” with Human Error Publishing
- Selected for inclusion in the Summer Anthology “Bards Poetry Review 2024”
- Pushcart nominee
- Exit 13 Issue, #29 publish “Tejas”
- Canyon Voices “The Heron” & “The Night Comes Quickly”
- Vietnam War Poetry December 2022 4 poems, April 2024 2 poems
- Spill Words Press January 2023, May 2023, August 2023
- Published in The Stillwater Review 2023
- Arts By The People December 2023
- Anthologies “The More I Forget” 2022, & “Nature Knows the Way” 2023
- Poetry Nation “Peace & Serenity” & “Retrospectively”
- Handbook for Savings in Freight & Logistics
- Working on a book for children titled “Fritz, My Bestest Friend”
- Over 60 Manufacturing Publications
- A Case Study at Lehigh University

- Active member of Newton NJ Writers Roundtable
- Active member of Poetry At The Barn
- Active member of Newton NJ Library writers and Poets

www.ingramcontent.com/pod-product-compliance
Lightning Source LLC
Chambersburg PA
CBHW022205160726
48282CB00024B/331
9788119654826